James Denney

Gospel Questions and Answers

James Denney
Gospel Questions and Answers
ISBN/EAN: 9783743395244
Manufactured in Europe, USA, Canada, Australia, Japa
Cover: Foto ©Lupo / pixelio.de

Manufactured and distributed by brebook publishing software (www.brebook.com)

James Denney

Gospel Questions and Answers

GOSPEL QUESTIONS

AND

ANSWERS

BY THE REV. PROFESSOR
JAMES DENNEY,

TENTH THOUSAND

HODDER AND STOUGHTON
PUBLISHERS LONDON

CONTENTS

I

THE QUESTION OF MISGIVING, . . 1
What lack I yet?

II

THE QUESTION OF DOUBT, . . 19
Art thou He that should come?

III

THE QUESTION OF FAILURE, . . 39
Why could not we cast him out?

IV

THE QUESTION OF POVERTY, . . 61
Whence should we have so much bread?

V

THE QUESTION OF REMONSTRANCE, .   PAGE 78

Goest Thou thither again?

VI

THE QUESTION OF AMBITION, . . 98

Who is the greatest in the Kingdom of Heaven?

VII

THE QUESTION OF FOLLY, . . 120

Are there few that be saved?

THE QUESTION OF MIS-GIVING

'What lack I yet?'—MATT. xix. 20.

MOST people would have envied the man who put this question to Jesus. He seemed to have everything that heart could wish. He had youth, which means hope and inspiration and an unknown inheritance in the future. He had social position, which usually tends to satisfaction with one's self. He had wealth, which attaches the soul so powerfully because it is on the borderland, as it were, of the material and the spiritual —not bad, if not good, but a permanent possibility of doing and of enjoying most things that men wish to enjoy or to do. He had character, too, which was better than all: he could hear the commandments recited by Jesus with no qualms of conscience. Neither rank nor wealth nor youthful passions had hurried him into any of those excesses which can never be forgotten, and which make memory a curse. But in spite of this extraordinary happiness, in spite even of his good conscience, his soul was not at rest. He felt that something was wanting; he could not say he had eternal life, and it was a divine prompting that brought him to Jesus with the question, 'What lack I yet?'

No situation is commoner in the Church than that of this man.

There are hundreds and thousands who have been brought up in Christian homes, and recognise more or less their own likeness in him. They, too, have kept the commandments all their life. There is no great stain upon their conscience that makes them hopelessly miserable. If they have not rank or wealth, at all events they know that it is not rank or wealth that would make any difference to them. They have been, as a rule, pure, truthful, kind, respectful to their parents, considerate of the rights of others, reverent to the law of God; but they are not satisfied. They know that at the very heart they are not right. They have religion, of a kind, but it is not the religion of the New Testament. They do not take it with rapture. The characteristic note of New Testament religion—its assurance, its confidence, its joy in a life which leaves nothing to be desired—is the very one which their voice does not command. They are perpetually asking, 'What lack I yet?'

Jesus answers the question with the utmost plainness. But the answer was in more than words. 'Fastening His eyes on him, He loved him.' He appreciated all the good there was in the man, and still more his wistful inquiry after a more perfect good. Christ and a young man, as Samuel Rutherford said, is a meeting not to be seen in every town, but it is a grateful meeting to the Lord. No one can be surer of Christ's interest and sympathy than one who comes with such a record as this ruler's to put the same question of misgiving. If there must be something peculiarly trying in the answer, Christ will flash His love into the heart before he speaks, that the questioner may know that the exacting words do not come at random or from want of feeling, but are inspired by a genuine care for his soul. But after the loving glance Jesus did speak, and that with all gravity. He did not pooh-pooh the man's misgivings, as unwise friends sometimes do. He did not say, ' This uneasiness of yours is morbid : it is an unwholesome mood which you ought not to indulge. Accept the responsibilities and the advantages of the position which God has given you, and do not worry or mope about ideals and impossibilities. Nobody can be more perfect than his nature and his place allow him to be; and it is a mistake to nurse what are really spiritual ambitions which forget what man is.' On the contrary, with His earnest, loving look fixed on the man, Jesus answered: 'One thing thou lackest. Go thy way, sell all that thou hast, and give to the poor, and thou shalt have treasure in heaven: and come, follow Me.'

There is no understanding this answer until we see that the pith of it lies in the last words, and that those which precede are only conditional. When Jesus says Follow Me, He implies that He has what the ruler lacks, and that the misgiving which troubled the ruler's soul was one which He, and only He, could overcome. This is the constant attitude of our Lord toward men; it is in this that we feel, first and last, how He is the Lord, and is conscious of being so. He stands over-against the world, and He knows that He has what all men need, and has it in such fulness that all men can obtain it from Him. This is the ultimate proof of His divinity, this is the infallible sign that He is Saviour: He can do for men, and for all men, what all men need to have done; He can give to men, and to all men, what all men need to receive; in His company, misgivings die, for He is the Author of perfection, of eternal life, to those who receive Him. There were men present when Jesus spoke who could certify that that was so. Peter was there, who had cried not long before, 'Lord, to whom shall we go? Thou hast words of eternal life.' John was there, who wrote long after, 'God hath given to us eternal life, and this life is in His Son.' This was what the ruler lacked, and it was to be had nowhere but in Jesus. Only through Him, through His words, through His revelation of the Father, through His coming death, through the Spirit which those who were His should receive, could he enter into a life in which misgiving should be no more. To sell all that he had and to give to the poor was for him, in the circumstances of the time, and with his moral constitution, the one condition on which it was possible to follow Jesus into eternal life. Jesus, in short, asked him to do what the twelve had done: 'Lo, we have left all, and followed Thee,'—at the same cost he should have the same reward.

Yet, although this is so, great emphasis is undoubtedly laid upon the preliminary condition: 'Sell all that thou hast.' Eternal life is not only the free gift of God in Jesus Christ; it has to be purchased with a great renunciation by every one who enters into it. He who lives in it, with a life from which misgiving has vanished, can not only say, as Paul said of his Roman citizenship, 'I was free born,' but also what Claudius Lysias said of his, 'With a great sum obtained I this freedom.' To put the same truth in another way, salvation is not only a gift, but a calling. Perhaps among Protestants it has been presented too exclusively as a gift. Men have been conceived as sinners *simpliciter*—as defeated, disgraced, doomed, in despair; eternal life for such must be a gift as pure and simple. But it is possible to conceive men also as seekers and aspirants. It is possible to find men in whom the inner life is characterised not by the sense of guilt, but rather by that of deficiency: whose souls do not cry with St. Paul, 'O wretched man that I am!

who shall deliver me from the body of this death?' but rather question gravely with this ruler, 'What lack I yet?' To these last salvation is a calling. Follow Me is the sound of a trumpet. It is an appeal to those who are capable of great actions: who are brave enough, honest enough, earnest enough, to renounce everything, to pierce through everything, that they may win Christ. If they can find it in their hearts to count the cost and pay, they enter into the life which is life indeed. And they have no misgivings as to whether they are saved by grace. None are readier than they to confess what they owe to Christ. None are readier than they to utter John's confession: 'God hath *given* unto us eternal life, and this life is in His Son.'

But the price has to be paid, and often it is staggering. It has to be paid by every one. 'If thou wouldest be perfect . . . follow Me': Christ says that to us all, but between the two parts of the sentence comes the condition which must be fulfilled before we can follow Him, and enter into life. It will vary in different men, but it would be very extraordinary if it were not, in many, connected with money. There is nothing, for reasons already suggested, with which so many spiritual perils are associated. There is nothing to the advantages of which we are more keenly alive, to the risks of which we are naturally so blind. Does anybody really believe that it is easier for a camel to go through the eye of a needle than for a rich man to enter into the Kingdom of God? Does any one realise the deceitfulness of the heart implied in a remark of St. Francis of Sâles, that in all his experience as a confessor no one had ever confessed to him the sin of covetousness? If there is anything in the teaching of Jesus, we may be sure that voluntary poverty—the deliberate renunciation of possessions—is the strait gate through which alone multitudes can enter into the Kingdom of God. Self-scrutiny would often reveal that the one thing an otherwise good character lacks is to be made right with God in this particular: to resign a source of income that He could not approve, to arrest a self-indulgent expenditure, and replace it by an unselfish spending for a good greater than our own; to bring money, in a word, under law to Christ. And when we look at society as a whole, the one conspicuous feature is, not simply the power of money, but the power of money organised and entrenched against the Kingdom of God. The vested interests of iniquity are the most gigantic social forces among which we live.

It is easy to protest against such ideas, and one can easily imagine the disciples themselves protesting. It was seldom they had the chance of enlisting such a recruit as this respectable proprietor, and they were certainly astonished, and probably disconcerted, at the exacting terms of discipleship proposed to him by Jesus. Many share their astonishment, and criticise the incident in the spirit of Strauss, who thinks that Jesus in His teaching fails to do justice to the instinct of accumulation. Jesus had no right, such persons say, to make the demand He did. God gave the ruler his property, not to squander it on so-called charity any more than on self-indulgence, but to administer it in His service. It is enough to reply that of this the ruler was the best judge, and his conscience sided with Jesus. Certainly, at the first hearing, the words startled him; one of the evangelists notices his sudden change of countenance; but he went away sorrowful. Not angry, as he would have been if the demand of Jesus had been a mere impertinence; but sorrowful, because he felt that Jesus had touched the secret infirmity of his character, and that he had not courage to face the cure. Could anything be more melancholy than to see a man whom Jesus loved, a man with a yearning after eternal life, drop his eyes under that loving, searching glance, and go away sorrowful— go away, although he wished to stay; go away, because he loved money better than the life of God; go away, with a more poignant ache in his heart than when he came to the Great Physician? It is one of the saddest things in the gospel, and how much sadder when we think of the look with which Jesus followed him—a man who, when it came to the point, counted himself unworthy of eternal life.

Let his very sorrow speak to us in Christ's name. It is the only experience in such cases. No one is ever glad that he has turned his back on Jesus. The things we prefer to Him lose their value the instant they are so preferred. The possessions of the ruler would never again be to him what they had been. The brightest sun that ever shone would never lift from his fields the cold shadow of that great refusal. He knew now what he lacked and how much it was. And if we want a companion picture to inspire, as this to awe us, let us look at St. Paul as he writes to the Philippians: 'Howbeit what things were gain to me, these have I counted loss for Christ. Yea verily, and I count all things to be loss for the excellency of the knowledge of Christ Jesus my Lord: for whom I suffered the loss of all things, and do count them but dung, that I may gain Christ, and be found in Him.' That is the life in which there is no misgiving more—the life that only God can give, in Jesus Christ His Son; the life, too, that every one has to buy, at the cost even of his money.

THE QUESTION OF DOUBT

'Art thou He that should come, or do we look for another?'—MATT. xi. 3.

THE Jewish race, more than any other, lived with its eye upon the future, and in this respect John the Baptist was the representative of his race. He believed in the Hope of Israel. He believed there was One who should come, a King and a Saviour, to do for the nation all that its noblest spirits had ever longed to see done. After He came, the final and perfect representative of God, there could be no other to look for; the history of Israel would have reached its term.

This great hope, which floated in the people's minds, waiting impatiently the appearance of some one whom it could claim as its champion, and whom it could invest in all the strength of a nation's faith, had been identified by John with Jesus. He had spoken of Jesus, while yet unknown to Him, as One mightier than himself, who could do what he had failed to do— baptize with holy spirit and with fire; he had consecrated Him to His life-work, as the instrument of Israel's hope, in baptism; he had seen heaven opened, and the Spirit of God descend and rest upon Him; he had borne witness that He is the

Son of God. Nay, by a sudden flash of revelation, as he looked upon Jesus he had seen that sin is not to be overcome, as he had tried to overcome it, by direct and violent assault, but by a method more mysterious, painful, sacrificial, even divine. Behold, he had said, as Jesus passed before him, Behold the Lamb of God, which taketh away the sin of the world.

It is this which makes the subsequent doubt of John so disconcerting; yet that doubt can be explained, if not justified. It is evident that John had somehow been disappointed in Jesus. The lofty witness which he bears Him, and which is recorded in the Gospels as the essential point in his relations with Him, probably represents the height to which John rose at the crises of his career, not the ruling quality of his thoughts. John belonged, we cannot forget, to the Old Testament, and his anticipations of the works of the Christ were shaped on Old Testament models, and on too partial a selection even of these. It would be wrong to say of one who was filled with the Holy Spirit from his mother's womb that he was an unspiritual man, but his hopes were of a cast which failed to do justice to the spirit of the new era. God's Kingdom must come, he thought, in a moment, suddenly; the axe that lay at the root of the tree would flash and smite; the fan would wave in the Judge's hand; in an instant the judgment would be consummated; the old order and its wickedness would be annihilated; the new would be set up, to last for ever. But John had not observed Jesus long till he saw that these anticipations were not destined to fulfilment, and the question inevitably rose Have I been right in attaching the hope of Israel to this Nazarene? Is He the Coming One of prophecy, or must our eyes turn again to the unknown future?

The crossing of hope and experience was aggravated in John's case by his own unhappy fortune. He had prepared the way of Jesus. Jesus had entered into his labours, had found in the circle of John's disciples every one of those who became His own most intimate followers, and yet to all appearance had forgotten him. All his services had not earned bare gratitude. As he pined in Herod's prison, and felt that power was still in bad hands, he could not but doubt whether the Kingdom of God had come in Jesus. It did not look like it. He might have been hasty in identifying the hope of Israel with Him, and he resolved to send two of his disciples to put the question point blank.

The answer of Jesus is of course an affirmative, but not in express terms. Not even to John the Baptist did He say, I am the Christ. The only religious convictions which are ultimately superior to doubt have to be attained in another way; they are revelations on the one side, and discoveries, or insights, on the other. They have little to do with Yes or No. When the doubt of John was submitted to Him, Jesus answered by exhibiting to John the grounds of His own certainty that He was the Messiah, the Hope and the Saviour of Israel. How did Jesus know Himself that He was the Coming One? What was the nature of that self-consciousness which certified to Him that He was the Sent of God, the Redeemer of men? The question has been much discussed by those who have written His life, but as far as we can make out the answer, it is here. 'Go and tell John the things that ye do hear and see: The blind receive their sight, and the lame walk, the lepers are cleansed, and the deaf hear, the dead are raised up, and the poor have the gospel preached to them.' These manifold blessings, bodily and spiritual, which were all one with the presence and work of Jesus upon earth, identified Him in His own mind with Him that should come. The features of the Coming One were adumbrated in those prophecies which had nourished His youth, and as He looked into them it was His own features that looked back upon Him from the divine page. Jesus recognised Himself in the great Servant of God, of whom it had been written, 'He shall not cry, nor lift up nor cause his voice to be heard in the street. A bruised reed shall he not break, and the smoking flax shall he not quench; he shall bring forth judgment in truth.' He recognised Himself again when He read in the synagogue at Nazareth, 'The Spirit of the Lord God is upon me, because the Lord hath anointed me to preach glad tidings unto the meek.' He recognised Himself once more, and the fruits of His work, in that bright vision of Isaiah xxxv.: 'Then the eyes of the blind shall be opened, and the ears of the deaf shall be unstopped; then shall the lame man leap as an hart, and the tongue of the dumb sing: for in the wilderness shall waters break out, and streams in the desert.' The correspondence between prophecies like these and that which He knew Himself to be, and saw around Him, identified Jesus to Himself as the Promised Saviour; He implies that the argument should have weight for John, and, with the proper qualifications, for us also. The argument from prophecy has been discredited by abuse; but the proper application of it—that which is made by our Saviour here, and which goes to show the fulfilment of the Old Testament in the New, or, in other words, the substantial unity of revelation—can never go out of fashion. The first generation of Christians was overwhelmed by its force, and the more it is understood the more highly it will be valued.

Thus far our Lord answers the first perplexity of John — that arising from his disappointed hopes. But when he adds, 'Blessed is he that shall not be offended in Me,' it seems almost certain that He refers to John's impatience with his fate. John could hardly believe the Kingdom of God was there, if he was left in prison. Jesus hints, in this warning word, that no man is too good to suffer for the Kingdom, and that no man should allow the necessity of such suffering to shake his faith in Him, and in the fulfilment of God's promises through Him. The continued existence and power of evil is a trial to Him as well as to us, but it did not shake His faith that God had visited the world in Him, to bless and save it, and it should not shake ours. It is dangerous to weigh our own importance against that of the Kingdom of God, and to argue that it cannot have come—that the hope of the world has still to be looked for —because we are neglected. Jesus knew that the Cross awaited Him, but that did not disturb His faith that the Kingdom had come in Him ; and He teaches more plainly elsewhere that the need of suffering wrong in its service, far from being a cause of doubt, ought to be a seal of faith.

The doubt of John is one of the most familiar religious phenomena of our own time. People look at the world, after all its long experience of the Gospel, and acknowledge a profound disappointment. 'Is the thing we see salvation?' Is Christ really the Saviour of men and of society? Or must we not, when we see the state of things around us, conclude that God has something better to do for the world than He has yet done, and that we must look on into the future for another? Especially when we see how spiritless and ineffective are many of the persons and institutions which carry the Christian name, must we not have doubts as to whether that name can really preside over the future development of the world, as it has no doubt done over much that is good in the past? Christianity certainly has been a power in history; but is it not a creed outworn?

Even in the Church the disposition to ask such questions

is strong. The shapes Christianity has taken, the institutions in which it has expressed itself, the ideals it has yielded, are subjected to unsparing criticism. Young people especially, those in whom 'the prophetic soul of the wide world dreaming on things to come' makes its power felt, those who look instinctively to the future as their home, yet desire guidance in it, can hardly help asking, Is Jesus Christ still the hope of the race? is it still at His lips we are to seek words of life?

Happily it can be shown that many of the most characteristic tendencies and hopes of the new age are distinctly Christian in their inspiration. It is a Christian principle which would lead in the state and in society to a more effective recognition of human brotherhood. It is a Christian principle which would try to secure for the honest age of labouring men and women a better abode than the poorhouse. It is a Christian principle which would aim at making every kind of human interest—politics, art, science, religion — accessible to all sorts and conditions of men; at guaranteeing, as far as possible, to every child of the human family his part in the common inheritance. It is a Christian principle, too, which would take care that no transformation of the social or political order should be made, whatever the economical gain to the many, which should involve injustice to the few; and which would provide against purchasing material advantages at a moral loss. Far from the prospect raising doubt under this view, it suggests one of the most solid and astonishing proofs of the truth of the Gospel. The ideal presented by Jesus Christ is always ahead of us, yet always adapted to our situation. He lived on earth nearly nineteen hundred years ago, and the inspiration of the world's progress still comes from Him. We have not passed this way heretofore, yet when we lift our eyes we see it is still He who is our guide. There are no new ideas in morals, no creative social thoughts, no wisdom of life, for which we have not to be indebted to Him. No: we do not look for another to bring in the world's hope.

And if we turn our eyes from the future to the present, and let the whole discouragement of it sink into our souls, we shall find again that our only hope is in Him. Sometimes it seems impossible to exaggerate the discouragement. Here are great towns, which have been Christian for a thousand years or more, and we know what they are. Is Christ the hope of the race, when after a thousand years' acquaintance with Him people still live in such houses, with such facilities for drunkenness and vice, with such a practical impossibility of being temperate and pure? Is Christ the hope of the race when, in a society which has known Him for thirty generations, there are whole classes that live by sin, and sell their souls to make their daily bread? Is Christ the Saviour of the world, when after all these centuries the world is manifestly not saved, and as far as great masses of society are concerned, is not the least like being saved? Here is the great cause of doubt and of heart-searching in those who have had hopes of what Jesus would do for men: here is the pain which makes them say to His face, 'Art thou He that should come, or do we look for another?'

Is it not wonderful that Jesus Himself had experience of this trial, and remained sure of Himself and of His divine vocation in spite of it? He saw, if we may say so, the failure of the Gospel. In this very chapter He upbraids the cities that had been spectators of His mighty works, yet had not repented. The way in which He overcame this trial was by looking away from the disappointments and failures to the work which was actually being accomplished and to the spirit in which it was being done. 'Go and tell John the things which ye do hear and see.' The big town with its misery and vice may be a melancholy sight; but look through it from end to end, search all ranks from the highest to the lowest, and you will be compelled to admit that the hopeful spots in it are those in which Christ is actually at work. Wherever you encounter a truly Christian man or woman you must acknowledge that there is one ray of light in the darkness, one grain of salt in the else unwholesome mass. It is not easy to understand that this is the way salvation works, that men should be so insensible, and God so intolerably slow; but it is easy enough to understand that if the Spirit of Christ were sovereign in all souls, the work of salvation would be done. Why then, because of the slowness of its conquests, should we look for another? Do we not read in the Book of Revelation, not only of the Kingdom, but of the patience, of Jesus Christ? Why should we doubt Him, because we have to share the trial of that patience? 'Blessed is he, whosoever shall not be offended in Him.'

THE QUESTION OF FAILURE

'Why could not we cast him out?'
MATT. xvii. 19; MARK ix. 28.

THE same page in the Gospel presents to us the glory for which man was created, and the humiliation in which he lives. We see Jesus transfigured at the top of the mountain, and at the bottom his disciples face to face with a possessed child they cannot heal, and taunted by the scribes whom they cannot answer. When Jesus descended, neither the scribes nor the disciples were forward to speak to him. The scribes became suddenly conscious of their inhumanity, for in their hostility to the followers of Jesus they had been indifferent to the sufferings of the child; the disciples were mortified by their failure; both were abashed in that gracious and mighty presence. The poor man, who alone suffered in his boy's suffering, explained the situation to Jesus. It was not flattering to those who had used His name. 'I spoke to Thy disciples that they should cast him out, and they were not able.' They were not able: there might be valid explanations, but there was the inevitable fact. Mark dwells on the struggle in the father's soul, on the paroxysm in the illness— epilepsy apparently—of the child, and on the wonderful words of Jesus about the power of faith.

It was only after all was over, and the crowd had dispersed, that the baffled disciples came to Jesus in the house, and asked, Why could not we cast him out?

This is a question which, whether we ask it or not, we have often to answer. The Church's failures are conspicuous enough, and there are plenty of indifferent or hostile spectators to demand the explanation of them. 'Why cannot you cast the evil spirits out of society, or even out of the members of your own body? Why are there men and women all about you, victims of evil passions and of evil principles, literally possessed by pride, by lust, by ill-nature, by drunkenness, by inveterate falseness? Why cannot you deliver them from the degradation and misery of vices like these?' Such questions are asked, but to such questioners they are never answered. The disciples, fencing with the scribes, did not yet know the answer, and even if they had known they might have found it impossible to tell. Nothing they could ever have told would have gone to the root of the matter. And it is always so. In any document which is of the nature of an apology made by the Church to the world—in any explanation of failure for the benefit of the non-Christian — the essential things are of necessity left out. There are explanations of a sort, pleas in extenuation more than enough, but not the truth. The truth comes out, not when the disciples are questioned by outsiders, but when they put this question to the Lord — Why could not we cast him out? The Lord's answer is its own evidence, and every man who has been conscious of failure in spiritual work will confess its truth.

'He saith unto them, Because of your little faith.' Jesus had spoken strongly to the father of the child about faith — 'all things are possible to him that believeth'; He had reproached the whole company as faithless and perverse; and now He explains by lack of faith the failure of the disciples. What is the faith on which He puts such stress? In a word, it is that exercise and effort of the human soul which lays hold of God, and brings Him into the field. It is that power in the soul which makes God present. To have no faith means to have no sense that God is here, no conviction that He is with us as a Redeemer from evil. To have little faith, like the disciples in this story, means to have only a feeble conviction that He is with us—a conviction that seems good enough as long as it is untried, but that vanishes or is reduced to impotence the moment we are confronted with the mighty forces of evil. With no faith, or with little faith—with no hold on God, or with a hold so slight that we faint and let go in face of the enemy—what can we do? We can do nothing. The power of evil in the world is a tremendous power: there is nothing to match it but the power of God. To overcome it is to work the mightiest of miracles, and it is God alone who does wondrous things. To go out to war with it without faith is to go out to certain failure, for it is to go out alone, without God. That is why men preach so often, and no one is blessed; and teach so assiduously, and no heart is won, even for ten minutes, by the love of God. We have left home to do it as if it were a simple thing; we stand before our congregation or our class as if it were a matter of course, and as a matter of course nothing is done. Why? Why, but because we are alone—because God is not here, present to our faith, to do what only He can do. In the time of James VI. there was a famous preacher in Edinburgh, Mr. Robert Bruce. 'No man,' says one of his contemporaries, 'in his time spake with such evidence and power of the Spirit. No man had so many seals of conversion; yea, many of his hearers thought that no man, since the apostles, spake with such power.' Do we not discover the secret of that power—a secret illustrating our Lord's answer to His disciples here—in the story told of his preaching at Larbert? He was in the vestry before the service, and some one was sent to call him. But the messenger brought back word that he did not know when the minister would come out. 'He believed there was somebody with him, for he heard him many times say with the greatest seriousness, "that he would not, he could not go, unless He came with him, and that he would not go alone,"—adding, that he never heard the other answer him a word. When he came out, he was singularly assisted.' That example explains to us, better than any words, the real cause of our failures. It is because we go alone to do the work of God. Why should we be able, without Him, to speak to the heart, to touch its secret springs, to call forth repentance, faith, love, self-surrender? Why should anything we say or do, apart from Him, have power to cast out evil spirits from men? We should be afraid to command them, even in the name of Jesus, except in the assurance that God is with us.

Only faith like this can enable us to overcome the fatalistic temper which is so apt at the present time to infect both those who suffer from evil and those who would help them. 'I am what I am,' a man says, 'and so I must be; there is a necessity in it against which it is vain to strive.' Even Christian men fall into this tone. They speak sometimes as if the evil we see were inevitable, and the enslavement of human souls by the devil a part of the order of the world against which it is useless, and indeed senseless, to protest. Such a recognition of natural law is equivalent to the denial of God. Faith means, in the last resort, the assurance that God can work miracles—that He is greater than all the powers of evil, and can overcome them even when they are entrenched in nature—that there is no connection formed in nature which He cannot break; nay, that He is *here*, in the omnipotence of grace, to do the very things which to nature are impossible. We need to believe in the spiritual nature and destiny of those we try to help: we need to believe that God is able, in spite of all that has been, to carry that destiny to a divine issue. 'Of all the sins that can be committed,' says the great preacher already referred to, 'I esteem this the greatest, when a man in his heart will match the gravity of his iniquity with the infinite weight of the mercy of God.' If there is a greater sin still, is it not that of resigning in apathy, as if thus it must be, the victory over God's sovereign mercy and holiness to the evil spirit which has subdued a human soul? If we want to see the victory where it ought to be, we must believe that there is One who is stronger than the strong man armed, and who can bind him and spoil his goods.

The Gospel of Mark enables us to see a little further into our Lord's meaning. There He is represented as saying, 'This kind cometh not out but by prayer (and fasting).' Faith has to be kept alive and vigorous if it is to work wonders, and here we see the conditions under which it lives. It was neglect of prayer, we should judge from this answer, which explained the dwindling of the disciples' faith.

Prayer, in the most general sense, is that exercise of the soul in which we come into God's presence and assure ourselves again of what He is in Himself, and of what He is to us. It is in this way the great proof of faith, and the great nourisher of faith; and it makes faith conscious of itself. There is no example of prayer, in the Bible or out of it, to compare with Jesus. He saw the evil that was in the world as no other saw it, felt it as no other felt it, was conscious as no other of the enormous strength with which it had rooted itself in the constitution of man and of society, yet He did not despair; His ceaseless passionate prayers kept Him always in contact with the omnipotent love of the Father. As He advanced to the most difficult works, He could say: 'I know that Thou hearest Me always.' *He* never failed.

Much work fails because it is not only prayerless, but in a manner an evasion of prayer. We bustle away with studying and preaching, with visiting and teaching, and after all it is ineffective and may even have been aimless: why? Because we have never had our work in God's presence to get guidance, inspiration, and force from Him. Prayer, to say nothing else of it, gives a new directness and strength to our purpose; it compels us to leave out of our methods all that is irrelevant, all that is of ourselves or looks to our own ends, all that is evasive: it compels us to go straight to the object in the strength of God. To think that we can do the work of God without prayer is to think that we can do it without God, and there can be no hypocrisy or presumption beyond that. Failure itself should have taught us to 'speak oftener of men to God, than of God to men.' Certainly it is only as prayer keeps our hearts right with Him, and enables us to address ourselves to our work, knowing that He is with us, that we can hope to see that work, which is His rather than ours, prosper in our hands.

The Revised Version leaves out the words 'and fasting' in Mark ix. 29. The scholars who agree with the revisers in this omission suppose the words to have been added—at a very early date—by some ascetically inclined copyist. I once heard a distinguished interpreter of the gospels say that he always felt 'and fasting' was unlike Christ, and that it was quite a relief to him to discover that there was good authority for omitting the words. But in spite of this, the question of evidence is not perfectly simple, and whether Jesus used the words on this occasion or not, they convey a truth to which

He often gave expression on other occasions, and which seems to me entirely in place here.

When we pray, in connection with any work we are about to undertake for God, we offer ourselves for His service: we put our whole nature and faculties at His disposal. We must be as fit as possible, to use the language of the gynasium, for the work He has to do. But fitness implies self-discipline; self-discipline implies abstinence, of various kinds; and the most general name for abstinence is fasting. Take the simplest case of all, the case of food. One need not speak of gluttony: nothing is more unholy than a glutton. But short of that, the man who has just dined heartily, and feels a little heavy with meat and drink, knows that many things, meanwhile, are impossible for him. He is too conscious of the flesh to be of much use spiritually: no evil spirits are likely to be dispossessed by him. Now there is a principle here which has a wide application, and it is this: that those who are going to fight God's battle in the world, to encounter evil and vanquish it, to succour the degraded and fallen, must vigilantly guard against any compromising relations with the enemy, and even with things otherwise innocent, which the enemy has been able to pervert to his use.

This is not an anti-evangelical doctrine. The fasting it commends is not a ritual abstinence twice a week, to be praised of men, but a voluntary abstinence, prescribed to the soul by itself, from all that it feels, though lawful otherwise, would impair its fitness for the service of God. If history can be summoned to prove anything, it is to prove that fasting in this sense is a *sine qua non* of successful work for God. The greatest of all preachers of liberty—St. Paul— never once enunciates the principle of liberty in its full compass without instantly subjoining to it this principle of restraint. 'All things are lawful for me, but—all things are not expedient.' 'All things are lawful for me, but—all things do not build up.' 'All things are lawful for me, but—I will not be brought under the power of any.' The principle of fasting is defended by every one of these 'buts': and experience shows that it is the men who have been superior to the attractions which life at the common level has for the average sensual man who alone have been able to do the world spiritual service. No doubt the explanation of much of our failure lies here. We are not separate enough from the evils from which we wish to save others. There is not enough of Puritanism in our moral ideal or in our character. We have not learned what Christ meant when he said: '*First bind the strong man*, and then spoil his house.'

Little faith, little prayer, little self-discipline: these are the things which spell failure in spiritual work. They are not the reasons we often hear. You are powerless, outsiders tell us, because your creed is too complicated, or because its forms of thought and expression are antiquated ; you are powerless, because your preachers have little intelligence, and little eloquence ; you are powerless, because you give too little (or too much) attention to æsthetics in your worship; you are powerless, according to the most recent diagnosis, because you are ignorant of social science, and do not care for the condition of the people. Perhaps if we wanted to excuse our failures, we might mention some of these things ourselves ; but if we want to understand them we had better hearken to Jesus. The evil spirits are not cast out, from want of faith, want of prayer, and want of self-denial, directed on our work as Christians. There is only one way to strength and success — re-union to God, and separation once more from the world.

THE QUESTION OF POVERTY

'Whence should we have so much bread?'
MATT. xv. 33.

WHEN the popularity of Jesus was at its height, great multitudes followed Him. The disciples, with their notions of what His Kingdom should be, saw in the crowds armies of possible supporters; to Jesus they were like shepherdless sheep, scattered and torn. He was moved with compassion for them, healed their sick, and day after day spoke to them of the Kingdom of God. As they lingered in His company, loth to take leave, and ill able, many of them, to face the journey home, He suggested to the disciples that they should give them something to eat. The disciples had a right to be astonished. They were poor men who had left their all to follow Him. They knew what hunger was, and had sometimes no more to stay their appetites than the ears of corn they plucked in their way through the fields, or the figs they gathered from a chance tree on the wayside. As they looked at the thousands crowding round their Master, and thought of their ill-furnished wallets, is it any wonder they asked, 'Whence should we have so much bread as to fill so great a multitude?' The question is virtually a disclaimer of responsibility.

The problem presented by Jesus to the Twelve is the problem of the Church to-day. The world lies before us, full of destitution, both material and spiritual; and its misery, if not its wistful waiting upon the Church, appeals to our compassion. The imagination is oppressed if we try to present to ourselves vividly the dimensions of its need. We cannot count the millions who are famishing for the bread of life; we cannot estimate the weakness, the misery, the lingering pain, the low vitality, the expiring hopes, the stupor, the vice, of those incalculable numbers. But if we see these things at all, and if we have learned anything from Jesus, His words will rise in our hearts, 'Give ye them to eat.' No doubt they have come to us again and again, and have probably been answered with the disciples' question, 'Whence should *we* have so much bread? What are our resources compared to the demands made upon us?' If the Lord made windows in heaven, and manna fell over all the earth, it would no more than meet the need. When we confront it with our paltry resources, it seems out of the question that we should attempt anything. Our five loaves are nothing among so many.

Jesus does not accept this disclaimer of responsibility. He feels so deeply for the crowd that He invokes the divine power to succour them, and the characteristics of the great miracles in which the bread is multiplied are a virtual answer to the disciples' question. We shall not be able to plead non-responsibility if we observe what these are : for they show how the seemingly impossible task is actually accomplished.

It requires, in the first place, the consecration to Christ, for His service, of all that we have. 'How many loaves have ye? Bring them unto Me.' This is fundamental, and till we have come so far it is idle to look beyond. Christ does not ask much, nor anything definite, but what we have. It is on the basis of the resources actually in our hands that the great task is to be accomplished.

This requirement applies to the material resources at our disposal. Many churches are crippled by financial difficulties, especially in their missionary work. Some of their members see the hungry multitudes, and are as eager to help as the love of Christ can make them, but the necessary means are not forthcoming. It is very rarely the case that this is due to poverty. There is plenty of money—no one knows how much—if only it were brought to Christ. Churches ought to feel, far more profoundly than they do, that avarice is a sin, and that there is nothing more repulsively unlike Christ than to weigh against the world's need of the gospel selfish indulgences of our own. If the wealth in the churches were consecrated as it ought to be—if it were ours only to be laid at Christ's feet—many aspects of our duty to the world would be much more practicable than they are.

The same holds good of spiritual resources. How few Christian people comparatively give themselves exclusively to the service of God in the gospel! How few men, especially from those classes in which it would imply the renunciation of a business, a fortune, or a career, give themselves to the Christian ministry! Surely there must be some whose hearts have been touched by the world's destitution, and have heard the Master saying: 'What hast *thou*? Bring it unto Me.' Let no man say that what he has is nothing to the need: that his infinitesimal quantity of knowledge, faith, hope, charity, could only mock the world's distress. It is with what His disciples have that Christ is going to satisfy the universal hunger, and He can do nothing till their whole store is at His feet. The necessity of the world appals us because the great mass of disciples will not bring anything: they are like non-effectives in an army, a burden, not a strength. In most churches women are far more loyal than men to the world's claims and to Christ's command. They put their spiritual resources as teachers, administrators of charity, visitors of the poor and the sick, far more freely at His disposal. But the force which the Church sends into the field is nothing to what it should be. It is nothing to what it would be if there was not one of her members who did not bring to Christ whatever he had. I suppose if the Twelve had reserved or saved any of their stores on this occasion, the miracle could not have been wrought: and certainly the world's needs remain unsatisfied, not so much because the Church is poor, as because she lacks that compassion and that faith in God to which the consecration of all she is and has would be easy. Why are we so slow to learn that all spiritual possessions are multiplied by use, and that, however it may be with gold and silver, the more we give the more we have of all that satisfies the hunger of the soul? It is spending, not saving, which is the way to wealth here.

Consecration of what we have, however little, is the first and most essential point of Christ's answer to the question, 'Whence should we have so much bread?' But to consecration He adds method. 'Make the men sit down by hundreds and by fifties.' No conceivable supplies could feed five thousand men pell-mell, and the women and children would be sure to be overlooked. The difficulty of feeding the multitudes has been aggravated by the haphazard fashion in which it has been attempted. Our own country is a conspicuous example of this. The want of method is seen in numberless evils. One is the mutual jealousy of Christians. Often they seem to contend with each other instead of with evil; they are more like merchants trying to cut each other out of a market than good men seeking in Christ's compassion to relieve human need. Another is the wrong ideas which the multitudes acquire of the gospel. They can hardly help thinking that they are being courted by rival churches, and instead of seeing in the gospel something which they deeply need, they are tempted to see in it only the private interest of some church or minister, to which they are willing to lend their patronage — for a consideration. Another is the waste which is inseparable from want of method. And another still is the tendency to evade responsibility. Churches are played off against each other: the Established Churchman is content if the people say they are Free, and the Free Churchman if they say they are Established; and neither then is so much concerned with the more serious question, whether they have received Christ. Want of method, generating all these evils, makes the resources of the Church far less adequate than they might be to the demands upon them; and method must be mastered if we are ever to give the multitudes to eat.

The miracle culminated in the thanksgiving of Jesus before the breaking and the distribution of the bread. The thanksgiving was evidently a characteristic and striking act. When John wrote his gospel, perhaps sixty years after, he referred to the scene of the miracle as 'the place where they did eat bread, *after that the Lord had given thanks.*' This was what stood out in his memory. The thanksgiving indicates the spirit in which alone anything can be done answering to this miracle. We can imagine that the disciples, as they lifted their eyes from the five barley loaves and the two small fishes to the hungry thousands on the green hill-side, were uneasy, alarmed, and not a little miserable; but Jesus was grateful and glad. That scanty store was the Father's gift, and it is as easy for God to feed five thousand

F

men as to make five loaves. Those very loaves sprang from His blessing upon the seed, and He who multiplies the grains in the ear can multiply all that we put at His disposal. When we bring what we have to Jesus, let us remember that it is not our own. If it were, we might disparage it, and calculate the disproportion between it and the need it has to meet; but it is God's gift, and though it seem a small thing, we are to rejoice in it as His. Our little store may seem ludicrous to others; they may laugh at our contribution of money or intelligence, of faith or love, to the world's necessities; but if we are grateful to God that there is at least this which we can offer for His service, it will multiply as we use it. It was so with the disciples; the bread never failed under their hands, and when the multitudes had eaten and were filled, their own baskets were full. They were richer than before they had given up their all.

Thankfulness is the only spiritual temper in which hope and joy can live, and without hope and joy we can never approach the multitudes for Christ. Perhaps the most signal illustration of it in Scripture is the thanksgiving of Jesus at the Last Supper: as He took the bread and the wine He gave thanks. Can we doubt that as He made them symbols of His body and blood His thanksgiving covered His own sacrifice for sinful men?

Can we doubt that He gave God thanks that it was His, in accordance with the Father's will, to give His life a ransom for many? Too often we regard the demands which are made on us by God and the world as a grievous tax: as long as we do so, no response we make to them can ever be equal to the world's need. But that need would not be beyond the Church's resources if Christians with one consent laid all they have at Jesus' feet; if they distributed the common duty among themselves; and if their hearts rose up to God in gratitude that He had called even them into the fellowship of His Son's ministry. If we could only learn these secrets, or rather attain to these virtues, we should know the answer to the question, 'Whence should we have so much bread to feed so great a multitude?'

THE QUESTION OF REMONSTRANCE

'Goest Thou thither again?'—JOHN xi. 8.

THE Gospel of John differs from the other three in showing us more of the Jerusalem ministry of Jesus. We could, indeed, infer from them that His relations with the capital had been more serious than appears from the surface of their narratives; the great cry, 'O Jerusalem, Jerusalem, how often would I have gathered thy children together as a hen gathereth her chickens under her wings, and ye would not,' is of itself sufficient to prove this. But the Gospel of John might almost be read as an illustration of this text. It exhibits the repeated efforts of Jesus to win the Jews, and the steadily growing antipathy with which these efforts were repelled. In the second chapter, at His first appearance, we are told that He did not trust Himself to them, knowing what was in man. At His next visit the Jews seek to kill Him, because He breaks the Sabbath and makes Himself equal with God. A little later the rulers send officers to apprehend Him; later still, the people take up stones to stone Him even in the temple courts. A renewal of this murderous assault compelled Him to seek refuge beyond Jordan, and it was there, apparently, that the message came to Him from Martha and Mary: 'Lord, behold, he whom Thou lovest is sick.' Perhaps the two days that He remained in Peræa encouraged the Twelve to think that He was now beginning to take care of Himself, and their amazement was all the greater when He said, 'Let us go into Judæa again.' It was putting His head into the lion's mouth, and they felt He might do it once too often. As Peter had done before at Cæsarea Philippi —though the precedent was not auspicious—they ventured to remonstrate. 'Master, the Jews even now were seeking to stone Thee, and goest Thou thither again?'

The answer of Jesus is striking. 'Are there not twelve hours in the day? If any man walk in the day he stumbleth not, because he seeth the light of this world. But if a man walk in the night he stumbleth, because there is no light in him.'

Practically the disciples had accused Jesus of recklessly shortening His life, and the answer signifies that the life which is spent in doing the will of God is always long enough. 'Are there not twelve hours in the day?'— a long, ample, gracious, liberal space of light to fill with work. Jesus does speak elsewhere of the shortness of time and the urgency of duty: 'We must work the works of Him that sent Me while it is day: the night cometh when no man can work.' With this idea we are familiar, but we need to habituate our minds to the complementary one, that for the faithful servant of God there is plenty of time, and no risk of life coming to a premature end. If we only did at each moment the duty which the Father has assigned to it, we should never be hurried nor confused; night would not overtake us; we should not stumble like the man who has to continue his journey in the dark; the true light would shine upon us till our day's work was done. And whether the life thus lived was short or long measured by human standards, it would be all that it need be to one who could say at last, 'I have finished the work which Thou gavest me to do.' For work, not time, is the measure of life.

The remonstrating question of the disciples is silenced therefore by a great confession of faith in God. 'My times are in Thy hand': so we read in the thirty-first Psalm, a psalm used by Jesus on the cross; and close by the words we read again, 'Fear was on every side; while they took counsel together against me, they devised to take away my life. But I trusted in Thee, O Lord; I said, Thou art my God.' One can hardly help thinking that the Psalm was in the Saviour's mind as He rebuked the timidity of His followers, and bade them remember the ever-present providence of the Father. Jesus is the author and finisher of faith in this providence, the Pattern of a trust in God so perfect that it leaves to Him without misgiving all that disquiets common men. It is God who fixes the length of our day. No enemy can reduce the twelve hours to ten or eleven, and no anxiety or evasion of our own could stretch them to thirteen or fourteen. Such faith is not fatalism—a stony acquiescence in whatever happens, as inevitably fixed by chance or by necessity; it is the loving acceptance of a Father's will, which we believe and know is seeking our good. It is this which gives serenity to life even when it is encompassed with peril. It is this which secures sunshine all through the hours in which our work is to be done. Every bitter word His enemies spoke against Jesus, as He hung on the cross, turned to His praise, but none more gloriously than this—He trusted in God. And of all happy expressions of His trust, there is none happier than this, when as He set His face for the last time to go to the city that killed the prophets, He said to His trembling followers, 'Are there not twelve hours in the day?'

Faith is the root of all the Christian virtues, and our Lord on this occasion, in contrast with His disciples, eminently illustrates two of these.

The first is courage. Jesus knew that He was going into danger; He foresaw, as the disciples did not, not merely the risk but the certainty of an ignominious and painful death. But He did not weigh His life against the Father's will, which called Him to Bethany. He counted not His life dear to Him that He might finish His course and the ministry He had received.

Courage is the most elementary of virtues, and perhaps there are few who are incapable of acquiring it in some degree. Soldiers acquire it in the simplest form, and it is readiness to surrender life at the call of duty that makes the soldier's profession not merely lawful, but great. Physicians and nurses, who have to do with infectious diseases, acquire it almost as simply and inevitably as soldiers. After all precautions, it remains for them to take their life in their hands; and the thousands who do so and would rather die themselves than leave the sick unattended are practising a Christian virtue. But it is Christian in a preeminent sense when it is practised in the interest of men's souls. The annals of missionary enterprise abound with examples of that very spirit which Jesus here seeks to infuse into His disciples. The men who have planted Christian churches along six hundred miles of the coast of New Guinea, among tribes whose sole trade had been to barter sago for earthenware pots in which to cook man, are illustrations of it. So are the men who have laid the foundations of the Church in the unhealthy regions of Western and Central Africa, and in many of the Pacific islands. But is their courage always appreciated? 'What!' do we not hear people say; 'are you going to carry the gospel to the Congo? Do you not know that the Congo is worse than Sierra Leone, which used to be called the White Man's Grave? How many people have died there already! Are you going there again?' By the inspiration of Christ men and women have been found to answer: 'Yes, we are going again. What is life for, but to be used in His service? We are ready to die, and to die on the Congo, far from help and friends, for the name of the Lord Jesus.'

These are exceptional or rather signal cases of courage; for virtue excepts no man from her claims. A Christian who has not this courage, in the measure in which his circumstances require it, is a contradiction in terms. When the Book of Revelation enumerates those who are shut out of the New Jerusalem, the very first title in the list is 'the fearful,'—that is, the cowards, who can brave nothing for Christ's sake. Whoever gets into heaven, they do not. Few people would plead guilty to cowardice in general, but how many have actually *exposed* themselves in the Christian Service—not to death, which is not an every-day affair, but to an uncivil word, a rebuff, an impertinent laugh, the pity of superior persons? Why are we not more visibly, more decidedly, Christian? Why do you not remonstrate with that man, who is your friend, and who is going wrong? Why do you not protest against the tone of conversation in that company which you frequent? Why do you not go on that errand, though you know it will be thankless, and may very likely provoke the coolness, the rudeness, or the contempt of others? Why do you *not* 'stand in jeopardy every hour'? Is it because you are afraid? Remember that cowardice is as incompatible with any Christian as with any natural virtue; and that if anything is alien to Christ it is this. He did not weigh life itself against duty: how can we follow Him if we are always balancing our own convenience, or rather our own indulgent selfishness, against the claims of God?

The other virtue conspicuous in our Lord's conduct on this occasion is patience. He was going back to Judæa, not merely for the sake of Lazarus, but for the sake of the Jews. In raising His friend to life again, He was making a last and supreme appeal to their unbelief. Again and again He had tried to win them already, and had been steadily repulsed: what was the good of trying further? So men might have argued, but Jesus did not. It was written of Him long before, 'He shall not fail nor be discouraged,' and the prophecy was illustrated when He resolved to give the Jews one opportunity more. The Apostle understood this when he wrote, 'The longsuffering of our Lord is Salvation.'

Is it not amazing, when we think upon it, the number of chances which God's patience gives to men? The number of times He visits us, hoping to find a kindlier welcome than He has yet done? Every morning as His sun shines upon us; every Sabbath as it speaks of His work as our Creator and Redeemer; every incident that breaks the thoughtless monotony of life and makes us feel beneath the surface; every word of God that leaps out on us from the Bible; every gospel sermon to which we listen —in all these Christ comes and comes and comes again. How often has He come to us? What does He come for? What reception does He get? If there were an angel standing by and looking on, might He not ask in amazement, as the disciples did on this occasion, 'Lord, goest Thou thither again? That man, who has heard Thy voice every day, and still loves the world, and will not follow Thee: that man who calls himself by Thy name, and affects reverence for the gospel, and defends the truth, but who is a cold - blooded, self - complacent Pharisee: that man, whose conscience has been touched, now more and now less keenly, any time these twenty or thirty years past, but who remains a coward, a sensualist, a slanderer, a thinker of low thoughts: Goest Thou to him again?' Yes, Jesus goes to him again. The grace of our Lord is exceeding abundant. He comes to us once more, this very moment; and if we remember how we have turned Him away already, and sulked, and made excuses, and stifled the heavenly voice, and counted the cost and found it too high, let the remembrance of these things humble us that His patient love may prevail at last. Remember that His longsuffering is salvation.

It is not only salvation, but a pattern and an inspiration for all Christian service. The most earnest are apt sometimes to fail and be discouraged, and they need to remind themselves that Jesus resisted such temptations. The Church becomes disheartened with great problems, like the maintenance of the Christian standard among its members, the defence of Christian truth, or the propagation of the gospel among the heathen; and when it is disheartened, it relaxes its efforts. Missionary operations are curtailed, and there is a weary acquiescence in what we know is not the best. It is the same with individuals. How many Sunday-school teachers have resigned their classes, because the boys and girls were irresponsive, or less? How many men have tried to save a comrade as he sank through the first stages of drunkenness, but when their efforts were repulsed resigned themselves not even to try any more to do him good? How many are so wounded in what they call their self-respect, but what is really their pride, by the first rebuff, or the first symptom of defective appreciation, that they wash their hands of all responsibility to others, and retire to keep a selfish state? If we call ourselves Christians, let us imitate Jesus. What if we are not appreciated: was He appreciated? What if we meet with ingratitude: were the Jews grateful to Him? Let us remember that the disciple is not above his Master, and go again and again and again—as He went to the Jews and as He has come to us —to the most inappreciative, the most thankless, the most irresponsive of men. Let us go in His spirit, brave and patient, and so full of love that no other motive can have place in our minds. Let us go with His words in our ears: 'O Jerusalem, Jerusalem, how often would I have gathered thee!' Let His longsuffering, which is salvation, have its perfect work in us. And then the faith in God from which these graces spring will be confirmed by them, and through all dangers and discouragements we shall walk in the light with Him and not stumble.

THE QUESTION OF AMBITION

'Who is the greatest in the Kingdom of Heaven?'—MATT. xviii. 1.

IN substance, if not in set terms, this question was put to Jesus again and again. The disciples were firm believers in the Kingdom, and had staked everything upon its coming. If they were ever to be great, it must be then; and it was natural enough for them to think that as they had shared the fortunes of the King while He was waiting for His inheritance, they should have some signal reward when He entered upon it. Jesus Himself says as much. 'Ye are they that have continued with Me in My temptations, and I appoint unto you a Kingdom.' But their misconceptions of the Kingdom are nowhere more plainly seen than in their ambition to fill the high places in it. The world's idea of greatness is simply carried over from the old life to the new. It hardly needs to be explained. It is the idea that greatness consists in immunities, in exemptions, in the power of compelling others to do us service; it is as old as humanity; it is fostered in every human heart not only by native selfishness, but by plausible reasonings, innumerable examples, and habitual indulgence. The disciples hardly thought of modifying this idea: all that concerned them was, who was to be the great one. The best way to appreciate the question is to notice the various occasions on which it was put, and the increasing plainness, vehemence, and even severity of Jesus' answer.

The first occasion is that recorded in the eighteenth chapter of St. Matthew. Jesus had lately shown special favour to Peter, James, and John, admitting them to see His glory on the holy mount. He had spoken to Peter of the keys of the Kingdom, and recognised in him some kind of eminence among the Twelve. Perhaps there had been some heart-burning over these or similar events when they asked Him point-blank, 'Who is the greatest in the Kingdom of Heaven?'

Jesus did not answer directly. He never does answer questions about individuals. He would not even tell Peter what was to become of John. It is nobody's business who is to be greatest, so far as that is a personal matter. What does concern us all is not who is to fill the highest place, but in what way eminence is to be attained. And nothing could be more beautiful than the manner in which Jesus met these jealous, ambitious, mistaken men. Nothing could illustrate more finely the terms on which He lived with them — 'familiar, condescending, patient, free.' He called to Him a little child, and set him in the midst of them, and said, Verily I say unto you, except ye turn and become as little children, ye shall in no wise enter into the Kingdom of Heaven. The 'verily' marks the answer of Jesus as one of the utmost seriousness, as well as the utmost sweetness. The gracious manner, the affectionate illustration, must not diminish the solemnity of the truth. The faces of the rival disciples are at that moment turned away from the Kingdom. Nothing less than a complete turning in the opposite direction, a complete renunciation of ambitious rivalry, can secure even admission. As for anything further, 'whosoever shall humble himself as this little child, the same is the greatest in the Kingdom of God.'

The first point to notice in this answer is its generality—whosoever shall humble himself. There is no respect of persons with God. Greatness in His Kingdom is not titular or official, but spiritual. There can only be one Prime Minister in Britain, but the highest rank in the spiritual world is open to all.

The second and principal point in the answer is this—the prime element of greatness in the Kingdom of Heaven is unconsciousness. The humility of the child consisted in the fact that he was not thinking of himself at all. He had no claims to make in Christ's presence; he did not stand upon his dignity; he did not negotiate for terms, or for a reward, when Jesus held out His arms and said, 'Come.' There is a sense in which this unconsciousness belongs to the perfection of all greatness: we admire it most when the great man is what he is, or does what he does, as unconsciously as a flower opens to the sun, or a vine bears the clustering grapes. It is a distinct abatement, for instance, even in the highest intellectual powers, when they show a face of pride and scorn to the weak. And if this is true of earthly things, how much truer is it of heavenly? The man who can stand face to face with Jesus, and all the time be thinking of himself—what he is to get, how high he is to stand, what distinction he may win, what terms he may make—has no promise of greatness in him. The whole foundation of it lies here, that when we see Him the thought of self dies. If we can be like the little child in His presence; if we allow Him to call us, lift us, bless us; if we simply trust ourselves to Him, making no claim, not having even the shadow of a claim cross our minds, but content to be with Him, and having no thought beyond that; then there is the basis in our souls on which greatness may be built. There is the promise of it at least, if it be not blighted by folly or pride. Christianity is revolutionary here, as on all fundamental questions. Jesus turns the world upside down, because it is wrong side up; He tells us that if we wish to be great, instead of setting our own image before us, magnified by ambition and fond hopes, we are to set Him before us, and in Him lose the thought of ourselves entirely. For here also the saying is true, that he who loses his life shall save it.

The disciples were not without the sense that there was something unworthy in their question, something alien to the spirit of Jesus. He was not ambitious, but meek and lowly in heart; He did not seek His own; yet they were conscious of His greatness. Once when they had been discussing this persistent question by the way, he asked them what they had been talking about, and they kept silence. They were ashamed to say to Him what they had been saying, evidently with considerable animation, to each other; and it was a sign that they were learning, though slowly. But the lesson was far from perfect, for before long two of the most advanced and sympathetic of the Twelve not only raised the question again, but put in, through their mother Salome, a claim to the coveted pre-eminence: 'Grant that these my two sons may sit, one on Thy right hand, and one on Thy left, in Thy Kingdom.' And the other ten, on whom the sons of Zebedee had tried to steal a march, were filled with indignation; for they, too, had their ambitions, and were by no means ready to take the lowest room meekly.

Jesus, as Bengel says, was then

dwelling in His passion : He was to have others on His right hand and His left before He entered into His Kingdom. The Cross was now full in view ; it awaited Him at the end of a few days, perhaps not more than ten ; and the passion of it throbs in His answer. It is as though He said to them, 'You wish for places beside the throne? They are to be gained as the throne itself is gained. They are open to you as they are open to all ; they can be won by all who tread the appointed path. The greatness of the King—the Son of Man in whom humanity comes to sovereignty over the brute forces of the world—is the greatness of consecration, of suffering, of service, of death. That is how

I win My throne. Are ye able to drink of the cup that I drink, and to be baptized with the baptism with which I am baptized?' And then He turned from the two to the whole company, and with an urgency all the greater that this was among the last lessons He could hope to give to the men on whom the future of His work depended, explained once more the nature of His Kingdom and of greatness in it. 'What you have in your minds,' He says in effect, 'is a kingdom of this world, in which the great people lord it over the lowly and the strong exact service from the weak; but My Kingdom is the very reverse of that. " Whosoever would become great among you, let him be your servant; and whosoever would be first among you, let him be your slave; even as the Son of Man came, not to be ministered unto but to minister, and to give His life a ransom for many."'

The greatness, then, which begins in unconsciousness—in the absence of any thought of self, or of what self may claim—is perfected in service; that is, in the thought of others, and of the needs of others to which we can minister. High in the Kingdom of Heaven is he who has learned from Jesus to put himself out of his thoughts, and to spend and be spent, to the utmost limit of means and life, in lowly loving service of others. The further we travel along this road, the nearer we come to the King in His glory. Ambition makes us look at men in other lights—as rivals we have to overcome; possible claimants on our help, of whom we have to steer clear; as tools to be used, and then thrown away; as insignificant counters—but ambition is not love, and only love can exalt in Christ's Kingdom. If we keep in His company, we shall attain that heavenly greatness, in some degree, which is fatal to selfishness and pride, and to which pride and selfishness are fatal.

Even the passionate lesson evoked by the ambition of James and John was not enough to cure the Twelve of their deep-seated fault. It broke out once more at the Last Supper, possibly over some small dispute as to places at the table, for the paltriest spark can kindle this kind of fire. Whatever it was, it had the usual effect; in thinking of themselves they forgot to think of each other. The odiousness of ambition is that it expels love, and when love is cast out men are blind to duty. There was no one to wash the disciples' feet, as decency and comfort required, and no one would confess inferiority by moving hand or foot to supply the deficiency. Then it was that Jesus gave a last lesson on greatness in the Kingdom of Heaven. In the full consciousness of His divine nature and dignity—knowing, as the evangelist says, that the Father had given all things into

His hand, and that He came forth from God and was going to God—He rose from supper, laid aside His garments, took a towel and girded Himself. Then He poured water into the bason, and began to wash the disciples' feet, and to wipe them with the towel wherewith He was girded. We are not, I should think, to suppose that this was a gratuitous service, a mere ostentation of humility, a parable in action for which there was no natural motive; the disciples' feet needed to be washed, and ought to be washed; and when they were too proud to serve each other, Christ made Himself the servant of all. To all His other teachings, to the constant example of His whole life, He added this special instance of service, which must have cut them to the heart. How their cursed pride had humbled them again, and how, once more, had the lowly ministering love of Jesus exhibited His divine greatness! And He did not leave the act to teach its own lesson; He explained it with unmistakable clearness and emphasis. 'Ye call me Master and Lord: and ye say well; for so I am. If I then, the Lord and the Master, have washed your feet, ye also ought to wash one another's feet. For I have given you an example, that ye also should do as I have done to you.' And then with redoubled assurance, as if of a lesson which, in spite of its apparent simplicity, it seemed all but impossible for the disciples to learn: 'Verily, verily, I say unto you, A servant is not greater than his lord.'

It is as though He implored them to consider that there is only one kind of greatness in the Kingdom of Heaven, that kind which He possessed, and which others could only learn of Him. Love, unconscious of self but always mindful of others, ever awake to their needs, ever ready to serve them in the lowliest modes of service, incapable of pretensions, of claims, of self-assertion: this is the one and only greatness which God can recognise. It is not akin to what the world calls greatness; it is the exact opposite of it, and that is why it is so hard to understand. Not he who has most servants is great, but he who does most service. To teach the world this lesson has been hard, yet we dare not say it has not been learned at all. When Jesus lived, the most ignominious object on earth was the cross; now the cross is the loftiest and most honoured of all symbols, and this change in outward appreciation marks to some extent a corresponding change, wrought by Jesus, in the common idea of greatness. We build our churches cruciform; we make jewels of gold and silver on the same pattern; princes give the Victoria Cross, or the Iron Cross, to their soldiers, in honour of self-sacrificing courage; the word that once spoke of nothing but infamy is now the most sacred and glorious in human speech, because Christ has identified it with the greatness of love. *He* is great, who, as an early Christian glossed one of the royal psalms, reigns *from the tree.*

And all true greatness is measured by nearness to Him. The common work of our life, the work by which we make our living, is exalted, and we ourselves rise in the Kingdom while we work at it, when we regard it, not as the instrument of our own fortunes, but as the divinely allotted calling in which we are to serve our brethren. It becomes great, and makes us great, in proportion as we can treat it as a partnership with Christ in His ministry to man. And few who have had even a remote contact with Christian ideas would deny that the truly great figures in humanity are those in which the spirit of the Cross has been supreme. Where do we find anything so great as that utterance of Moses: 'Oh, this people have sinned a great sin and have made them gods of gold. Yet now, if Thou wilt forgive their sin—; and if not, blot me, I pray Thee, out of Thy book which Thou hast written'? Where do we find anything so great as this, unless it be in the similar yet more passionate and profound exclamation of St. Paul: 'I could wish that myself were accursed from Christ for my brethren.' These, as a great theologian has finely said, are 'sparks from the fire of Christ's substitutionary love.' And it is men like these whom that fellowship in the Lord's passion raises to His right hand and His left in His Kingdom.

THE QUESTION OF FOLLY

'Are there few that be saved?'—LUKE xiii. 23.

THIS question may no doubt be asked from different motives. Sometimes it has been forced upon men by the rigour of the theological systems in which they have been educated. 'By the decree of God,' says the Westminster Confession, 'for the manifestation of His glory, some men and angels are predestinated unto everlasting life, and others foreordained to everlasting death.' 'These angels and men,' it proceeds, 'thus predestinated and foreordained, are particularly and unchangeably designed ; and their number is so certain and definite that it cannot be either increased or diminished.' Calvinism is strong because, when necessity and chance are offered to it as the alternative explanations of the universe, and even of man's destiny, it elects for necessity ; but a statement like this is not required by any religious interest, and it stimulates a curiosity which may become a pain and a torment, but can never obtain the kind of satisfaction it seeks. There is no list published of the citizens of heaven, as there is of those who possess the franchise here. Others, again, ask this question in the perplexity of love. They look at the world, perhaps at themselves, or their own family or friends, and cannot but have misgivings. They are not sure that those who are dearest to them are in the way of salvation, and they are certain that multitudes are not. May not the way, after all, be wider than they had supposed? May not God have, among the forces working for redemption, some that are unknown to them, and that only produce their effect in the world unseen? Others may have the question prompted by the words of Jesus Himself. It seems to have been in some such way that it occurred, if not to the man who put it, then to the evangelist who records it. Luke has just set down the two parables which predict the extension of God's kingdom: it is like a mustard seed which expands into a great tree; like a piece of leaven which leavens a great mass of dough. The contrast between this glorious prospect and the actual fruit of Christ's labours reminded him of this question, as it may have put it into the questioner's own head at first. Nevertheless it is a foolish question. When it comes from the head it always is so; only when the heart lends it its tenderness and anxiety can it be profitably asked. And Jesus treats it as a foolish question: He does not respond to the speaker's curiosity or speculative interest; turning away from him to the others who were present, He says: 'Strive to enter in at the strait gate;

for many, I tell you, shall seek to enter in and shall not be able.' It is the same word, no doubt, which we find in a fuller form in the Sermon on the Mount: 'Enter ye in at the strait gate, for wide is the gate and broad is the way which leadeth to destruction, and many there be which go in thereat; because strait is the gate and narrow is the way that leadeth unto life, and few there be that find it.'

Question and answer alike recognise, what is recognised by every unsophisticated conscience, that there is such a thing as salvation, and that it cannot be taken for granted. In other words, what is put before us in this life is an alternative. There are two gates, two ways, two goals, two sides of the throne, two kinds of foundation for the house we build: and we have to make our choice between them. We can go in at the strait gate, or at the wide gate, but not at both. We can travel in the broad way or the narrow way, but not in both. We can build on the rock or on the sand, but not on both. We shrink from making this decisively plain to ourselves, that the decisiveness of our action or inaction may also remain veiled ; but it is implied even in this foolish question ; it is emphasised in our Lord's answer; and it is the one conviction without which thought on this subject is fruitless. The ideas we have formed of salvation and perdition, of life saved and life lost, of the bright banqueting-hall and the outer darkness, of heaven and hell, may be erroneous enough; but there can be no reason for thinking of such things at all, and as little profit in it, unless we feel that in the very nature of the case these are alternatives which for ever exclude each other. Christ's answer bears directly on this, and is wholly plain and practical. 'Strive to enter in at the strait gate.'

The strait gate, as we see from the Sermon on the Mount, is so called in opposition to the wide gate, and the wide gate is not so hard to understand. A wide gate is one through which you can pass easily, carrying what you please, and no questions asked. That, Jesus tells us, is the kind of gate which opens on the way that leads to destruction. Anybody can go in, and take what he likes along with him. You can go in with your money, your pride, your sloth, your appetites, your vices, whatever you please. Nothing is excluded, and there is no toll. The consequence is that many do go in. The wide gate is always busy; the broad way thronged with travellers. You can drift in with the stream, you can have the pleasant sense of being well supported, you can maintain a certain self-respect by pointing to the large numbers of people, of all possible capacities, tastes, and characters, who have taken that way. Nevertheless, it leads to destruction. Its very breadth and easiness prove this. Conscience is not only quite decided and unambiguous on the first point, that there is such a thing as salvation, and that it cannot be taken for granted; it is as decided and unambiguous on the further point, that while you may drift to perdition you cannot drift to eternal life. No matter how false our ideas may be as to the precise import of salvation or ruin, we have a witness in ourselves that Jesus speaks truth when He says that it is easy to be lost, and not easy to be saved; that you can be lost without an effort, but if you are to be saved, must summon up every atom of resolution.

What, then, is meant by the strait gate which opens on the path of life? It is a gate, as the name suggests, which excludes much. You can carry a thousand things to hell which you must lay down before you can take the first step on the way which leads to heaven. In one sense it is wide enough: it can admit any man; it can let the whole human race pass through, if they come one by one, and strip at the outside; but it is not wide enough for anything else. The question has sometimes been asked, 'What, in one word, *is* the strait gate?' and various answers have been given. It has been called Repentance, Faith, Christ, and what not. Even if these answers are in some respects true, as they are, they are misleading; they divert the mind from the very point which Jesus wishes to emphasise. His purpose is to make us feel that the entrance to the path of life is an entrance in front of which man becomes suddenly, profoundly, perhaps startingly conscious, that if he is ever to pass through *there* he must leave much behind him. If there is one word which expresses this, it is Renunciation. The strait gate is the gate of renunciation, and it is left for every man to say what in his case must be renounced before he can enter. No sin can go through: the strait gate calls for repentance, and renunciation of evil. No sham can go through: it demands renunciation of acted insincerity, and a humble resolve to walk in the truth. No compromising relations with evil can go through, no tenderness for old associations which ignore God, no disposition to fret or pity ourselves; and hence for some there is no entrance unless they pluck out a right eye, cut off a right hand or a right foot, and enter halt or maimed or blind rather than stay outside. To come to the strait gate is to feel that what lies beyond is the one thing needful, and that it is a good bargain, for the sake of it, to renounce all that has ever been dear to us.

Jesus takes it for granted that every one has something to part with. The gate is a strait gate for all who go up to it. There is not a man on earth who can be saved as he is: he has something to renounce before he can enter into life. This is one of the indirect ways in which Jesus assumes the natural sinfulness of the human heart. The heart may have the capacity of heroism, and of making the great renunciation which is required; but no heart is spared renunciation; no man enters the Kingdom without the sense of sacrifice and constraint. And it is because the renunciation is painful and requires a great effort, that Jesus says with such solemnity and urgency: '*Strive* to enter in at the strait gate; for many, I say unto you, shall seek to enter in and shall not be able.'

Strive to enter in: is this what everybody does, whom God in His grace brings up to the strait gate? Unhappily not. Some, when they come face to face with it, and understand in the depth of their hearts the renunciation it requires of them, simply withdraw. They will not think of entering at such a cost. Others hesitate, and stand hesitating for years, perhaps for a lifetime. They are in two minds about going in till their dying day. The blessings of the heavenly kingdom, the company of Jesus, and the new life, are very real to them, and very dear; they so crave the enjoyment of them; but the things they must renounce are also very real and very dear; and they cannot win from themselves the irrevocable sacrifice, and go in. Others, again, to an ordinary observer, are even more promising. They admire the life beyond the strait gate; they extol those who have paid the price and forced their way in; they take themselves a hasty timid step, now and again, in the direction of the door; but they remain outside. All such persons are in view when Jesus says, 'Many shall seek to enter in, and shall not be able.'

At first this seems a hard saying, and terribly unlike what we mean by 'the gospel.' The gospel is all grace and generosity: its characteristic word is, 'Him that cometh unto Me, I will in no wise cast out.' Why are there some, why are there many, unable to enter in, though they seek to do so?

Partly, no doubt, as Jesus goes

on to explain, because they do not seek entrance till it is too late. How ominous is that double 'begin' in Luke xiii. 25, 26! What a time to begin to think of entering—when the Master of the house has risen and shut-to the door! Is a man to keep God and the universe in everlasting suspense? Is the world to wait for ever to see whether I will make up my mind? If not, there is the possibility of beginning too late: of refusing to be serious till the door is shut, and seriousness no longer avails. 'To-day, if ye shall hear His voice, harden not your hearts.'

Delay becomes fatal, because it begets irresolution, and nothing more easily than irresolution becomes chronic, incurable, irreparable. Decent people probably lose more by it than by all the sins they confess put together. They lose eternal life by it when it makes them, as it eventually does, incapable of the grand decisive renunciation by which alone we can pass the strait gate.

Many, again, are unable to enter, because instead of accepting the conditions which the strait gate imposes, they try to get these conditions modified. They spend infinite time and pains trying to transact, to negotiate, to compromise with Christ. The gospel abounds in unqualified statements and in peremptory demands; such and such things, Christ tells us, are impossible; such and such others are necessary

—they simply must be. Many waste life, like incompetent men of business, trying to evade the inevitable, to achieve the impossible; they exhaust their talent in attempts to qualify our Lord's inexorable words; they seek, so to speak, to widen the strait gate, before they make any push to enter. They would fain justify their retention of something upon which the door closes, and in sophisticating conscience, and arguing against Christ's ultimatum,—the end comes and the door is shut.

But above all, many are unable to enter because they will not make the effort they could if they were wholly in earnest. Many shall seek, Jesus says; but His commandment is not seek, but strive. 'Strive' is much the stronger word; it is the word appropriate to a contest in which all the force of man is exerted against an adversary. Well-meaning people, as we say, will seek to enter in; but eternal life, our Lord tells us here, is the prize not of the well-meaning but of the desperate. Put all your strength into it when you come to pass the strait gate: it will need it all. 'The Kingdom of Heaven suffereth violence, and the violent take it by force.'

Such is the answer of Jesus to the idle, or at least in this case the idly put question: 'Are there few that be saved?' It is hard to be saved, it is easy to be lost, as experience shows. Jesus does not answer as knowing some divine decree which fixes men's destiny irrespective of their will; He answers out of His own sad observation of men's deliberate and voluntary conduct. He saw with His eyes many entering in at the wide gate, and travelling at their leisure, or at reckless speed, down the broad way; He found few who had it in their hearts to make the needful renunciation and to follow Him. It is throughout simple, stern, unquestionable fact in which He deals. No doubt many, when this question rises before them, look away from the present disheartening world, and speculate on the possibilities of salvation in the unseen; some can even assert roundly that sooner or later all shall be admitted to the light and joy of heaven, and can be indignant and almost contemptuous to those who do not share their confidence. But can we help feeling that to enter on this line is to ignore not only the testimony of experience, but the testimony of Jesus; and that conclusions which require us to treat the words of our Lord and the facts of life as things that must somehow or other, we cannot tell how, be got over, are not conclusions on which one dare venture much either for this life or for that which is to come? Jesus refuses to look at the question of salvation except in connection with man's responsibility and action. Many, He sees with pain, yet cannot help seeing, enter on the way that leads to destruction; many also, He sees with pain as keen, refuse to make the effort which is needed to enter into life. These are facts which consist with God's character, and no appeal to God's character can alter them. If a man is on the wrong side of the strait gate, it is not because God has shut it in his face, but because he is keeping something which can never go through.

The severity of our Lord's words about the strait gate is indeed mitigated in two ways. There is nothing Scripture teaches more plainly than the truth, which the heathen also had discovered, that though it is hard to become good, it is easy to be good. The initial difficulty in Christianity is the supreme one. Everything is unexacting compared with the entrance on the way. Christ's commandments are not grievous. His yoke is easy and His burden is light. 'A life of self-renouncing love is a life of liberty.' Even from outside the gate we can see this; it is the joy set before us to enable us to make the hard renunciation.

And the second lightening of the prospect is found in our Lord's express teaching, in this very connection, that hard as it is to enter into life, many will be found there whom men in general did not think to see. 'They shall come from the East and the West and the North and the South, and shall sit down with Abraham and Isaac and Jacob in the Kingdom of God.' The true Church, if these words are true, must be to a great extent invisible: 'the Lord knoweth them that are His,' and in every nation He has those, unknown to us, who have counted the cost and passed the strait gate into the everlasting Kingdom.

THE END

www.ingramcontent.com/pod-product-compliance
Lightning Source LLC
Chambersburg PA
CBHW031501160426
43195CB00010BB/1055